AF732702

ANDY DE JONG

THE KINGDOM EQUATION

LEADER'S GUIDE

Acknowledgements

We are grateful to Mr. Andy De Jong, pastor of Covenant Life Church in Grand Haven, Michigan, for writing this leader's guide.

We are also grateful to Dr. John Timmer, pastor of Woodlawn Christian Reformed Church in Grand Rapids, Michigan, for writing the student text for this course.

The Scripture quotations in this publication are from the HOLY BIBLE, NEW INTERNATIONAL VERSION. Copyright © 1973, 1978, 1984 International Bible Society.

Copyright © 1990 by CRC Publications, 2850 Kalamazoo SE, Grand Rapids, Michigan 49560.

All rights reserved. With the exception of brief excerpts for review purposes, no part of this book may be reproduced in any manner whatsoever without written permission from the publisher. Printed in the United States of America.

5 4 3 2 1

ISBN 0-930265-88-2

Contents

Introduction

The Kingdom Equation is a course that explores the parables that Jesus told to teach his listeners about the kingdom of God. The twelve-chapter text which this leader's guide accompanies was written by John Timmer, pastor of Woodlawn Christian Reformed Church in Grand Rapids, Michigan. Timmer challenges adults and young adults to see the parables as windows through which we gain insight into the unfamiliar world of God's kingdom on earth, as well as stories that call our values into question and shockingly reverse our typical human standards.

Many Christians, asserts Timmer, have mistaken or limited notions of what parables are. They think of them as earthly stories with heavenly meanings, as illustrations, as allegories, or as a stories with a single point. But all of these definitions diminish the true value of Jesus' teachings.

To truly understand Jesus' parables we must view them as metaphors. The parables equate familiar human scenes with the unfamiliar kingdom of God, thereby giving us a glimpse of the strange and difficult truths about God's kingdom. They are "kingdom equations."

The twelve challenging sessions of this course were developed

1. to lead participants to a truer understanding of the parables
2. to introduce Jesus' parables in a reflective, emotive manner
3. to place the parables in their cultural settings
4. to help participants use the parables as windows through which they can see God's kingdom.

Using the Textbook

All group members should have a copy of the textbook *The Kingdom Equation* by John Timmer. Reading the chapters of this book at home each week should be required. Without mandatory readings, group sessions will flounder.

You may wish to schedule an introductory session in which you distribute the textbook and briefly explain what you will be discussing together during the twelve sessions to come. Ask participants to read chapter 1 before your next session together.

Leader's Role

This course emphasizes group participation and discussion. A typical session will be less of a formal, structured "class" and more of a group of adults meeting together for discussion. You and the others will be learning together.

You'll notice immediately that the sessions in this book contain more discussion questions than you'll be able to cover in a typical forty-five minute group session. Our intent is not to frustrate you, but to provide you with an abundance of material from which to choose. This means, of course, that you'll be ignoring some of our questions; we also encourage you to change or replace questions and to use your own approach to leading some of the sessions. In short, we hope that you use this manual more as a resource than a recipe.

To help you prepare to lead each session, we have included sections of introductory and background comments for the leader. In these sections you will find material that will give you some different background and new perspectives on Timmer's chapter and on the parable in general. Reading through this commentary, in addition to the comments interspersed with the discussion questions, should help prepare you to direct the group's discussion in a meaningful way.

You will notice that each session is divided into a number of Focus sections. Under each Focus you will find suggestions, background commentary, and discussion questions. Use as many of the comments, questions, and ideas as seem appropriate for your group and your situation. Remember to encourage participants to ask their own questions, too, and try to answer these questions together as you work toward understanding the parable.

After the opening two sessions, which serve as an introduction to the course, we suggest that you begin each session with a reading or a telling of the parable that you and the group will be focusing on that day. Consider asking one group member to prepare this oral presentation each week.

We encourage you to close each session by inviting group members to meditatively and prayerfully respond to what they have learned from Jesus' parables.

Evaluation

As leader, you would do well to ask the group from time to time, "How are we doing?" Give people a chance to react to your use of group time and to the textbook. Is there anything they would like to do differently? Is there anything they would like repeated because it struck them as particularly meaningful or effective? Be candid and open with the class as you discuss how the sessions might be improved.

We, too, would be interested in hearing how your group is doing. We invite you to send your reactions, suggestions, or questions to:

The Kingdom Equation
Education Department
2850 Kalamazoo SE
Grand Rapids, MI 49560

SESSION ONE

What Are Parables?

Introductory and Background Comments for the Leader

The first two chapters of Timmer's book, *The Kingdom Equation,* introduce us to the world of parables as metaphors. Timmer builds a case for regarding Jesus' use of parables as metaphors in order to launch readers into a new perspective on Jesus' teachings. Through studying this book, we will learn to hear the familiar parables of Jesus in a fresh way.

Purpose of the Study

In this session the group will review the various ways in which people view the parables of Jesus. Special attention will be given to Timmer's case for viewing parables as metaphors. The session also leads participants to observe how parables as metaphors function in our thinking about the kingdom of God.

■ Focus 1: *Listening*

Welcome everyone to the class and attend to introductions and other preliminaries.

To set the stage for a discussion on this chapter and the chapters that follow, you may wish to start this first session with a story and a prayer, as follows:

Story

On a warm and sunny day in Chicago, two friends met on Michigan Avenue for lunch. It was the noon hour, and the sidewalks were jammed with people—some just enjoying the weather and others scurrying around, looking for a place to eat. The street was busy too, humming with buses and cars.

Walking down the sidewalk, Friend 1 commented to Friend 2, "Did you hear that?" Due to all the competition of noises, Friend 2 wasn't sure what Friend 1 was referring to. "I'm not sure what you're hearing," Friend 2 said.

"A cricket!" answered Friend 1. "Did you hear a cricket chirping just now?"

Somewhat puzzled, Friend 2 responded, "No. I can't say I heard a cricket above all this noise."

Friend 1 moved towards a planter that rested near the door of an office building. Pushing aside the foliage, he revealed a tiny cricket scurrying about in the dirt.

"That's remarkable," Friend 2 said. "I'm amazed that you could hear the tiny sound of that cricket above all this noise."

"It's not really so remarkable," Friend 1 commented. He reached into his pocket and pulled out a handful of change which he dropped onto the busy sidewalk. About a hundred people stopped dead in their tracks and gazed to the concrete below, searching for the coins that had hit the walk. Friend 1 stooped down to pick up his coins and said to his bewildered friend, "You see, it all depends on what you're listening for."

Prayer

"Dear Father in heaven, above all the noises that compete for our hearing, give us a longing to hear your voice, clearly and fully. Grant that the noise of our old worn-out ways of thinking about you may give way to the voice of new insights, leading us to praise and honor you with renewed hearts. Make clear what is unclear and refresh us through your Spirit. In Jesus' name we pray. Amen."

■ Focus 2: *Continuum*

The continuum exercise described below will tell you something about present perspectives or opinions about parables within your group and will help you measure changes in thinking throughout this course on parables. Try to make this exercise as non-threatening as possible, acknowledging the need to respect each other's opinions.

Before class make five different signs and hang them on the walls around your meeting room. The signs should read "Strongly Agree," "Agree," "Neutral," "Disagree," and "Strongly Disagree" and should be arranged on the walls in that order. Ask the group to respond to each statement that you read by placing themselves physically below the sign that most aptly describes their "position." (You may prefer to have participants remain seated and indicate where they "stand" by a show of hands.)

Read the following list, feeling free to add or delete statements as you see fit:

1. I understand what is expected of me in this exercise. (Hopefully everyone will stand under the sign "Strongly Agree.")
2. I have always thought that Jesus' parables were illustrations, much like the stories a preacher uses in his sermon to demonstrate a point.
3. I have been taught to believe that parables are earthly stories which have a heavenly meaning.
4. I believe that Jesus' parables are allegories in which everything stands for something else.
5. I believe that Jesus' parables make only one single point.
6. I believe that parables are metaphors that contain numerous possible ways of looking at something.
7. I believe that Jesus told parables because he knew how much people simply liked a good story.
8. I believe that Jesus told parables in order to separate the believers from the nonbelievers in his audience.
9. I believe that Jesus told parables so that his listeners would work harder at understanding the kingdom of God.
10. I am looking forward to this course and what I might learn from it.

Thank participants for their willingness to move about the room (if you used that option) and their boldness in declaring where they "stand" on the parables. Then ask the group to return to their seats.

You may want to open the discussion at this point to comments and questions people may have about the exercise and/or Timmer's explanation on various ways of interpreting parables. Take time to expand briefly on number 10, too, asking group members what expectations they have for this course and summarizing some of your own goals for the next eleven sessions.

■ Focus 3: *Metaphors*

Spend the remainder of your session discussing parables as metaphors that help us see the truth more clearly. Since much of Timmer's material may be new for group members, take time to clarify how a metaphor functions, talking together about some of the following points:

1. *A metaphor is a way of describing something unfamiliar by connecting it with something familiar.* Ask the group to think of some examples of familiar things to which Jesus compares himself (door, vine, way, truth, light, bread, water, shepherd) and God's kingdom (mustard seed, merchant looking for a pearl of great value, yeast, sprouting trees, and so on).
2. *Parables as metaphors often grab our attention because of their shock value.* Invite the group to mention some parables that jolted Jesus' audience and to explain why his perspective was so unusual. (For example, he told the parable of the Pharisee and the Publican to religious leaders who were "confident of their own righteousness and looked down on everybody else"; he told of a master commending an unjust steward and of a woman tearing her house apart to find one coin.)
3. *Jesus uses parables as metaphors to teach his listeners something about the kingdom of God.* He presses them to rethink their idea of *kingdom* and to apply this thinking to their involvement in the kingdom. He knows how difficult it is for them to understand his upside-down kingdom in which the last are first and the meek inherit the earth, so he tells them parables that use familiar images to teach them about the unfamiliar kingdom of God.

Again, take time to talk about a few examples together and to make sure all participants have a clear idea of what Timmer means when he describes parables as metaphors. You may want to explain that, much like glasses help us focus on the world around us, Jesus' parables help us focus on his kingdom.

■ Focus 4: *Closing*

In conclusion, remind the group to read the second chapter in preparation for the next meeting.

Close with a brief prayer, committing the group and their discussion to God's leadership and care.

SESSION TWO

What Is the Kingdom of God?

Introductory and Background Comments for the Leader

Chapter 2 focuses on the kingdom of God. The author wants to impress upon his readers that Jesus' parables point to God's kingdom and invite people into kingdom-centered living. Part of thinking about the kingdom is recognizing the lordship of God and of Jesus Christ over all parts of our lives.

This session will consist of two primary discussions, followed by a brief commentary on the short parables at the end of Timmer's second chapter.

Purpose of this Study

The group will first focus on Isaiah 40, a passage that leads us to see God's grandeur, noting that God stands in and over all creation and permits no other god to occupy the center of creation.

Next, the group will consider a number of questions centering around the theme of the kingdom of God. This discussion will help participants recognize the importance of thinking about and living a kingdom-centered life.

Finally the group will review Timmer's comments near the end of chapter 2 on three short parables. These parables clearly reveal how Jesus used ordinary, familiar things to teach his listeners something about God's kingdom.

■ Focus 1: *God's Kingdom*

Open the session with a word of welcome. Then turn to your copy of *Our World Belongs to God*, a contemporary testimony of faith found in the back of the new *Psalter Hymnal* or in a separate booklet published by CRC Publications. If you can only manage to come up with one copy of this testimony for your group, consider putting the recommended reading on an overhead or making photocopies for participants.

To set a worshipful tone for this session and to help focus the group on the kingdom of God, we recommend reading sections 7 through 13 in the testimony, the segments that focus on creation.

To close your session today, you may want to return to the testimony and read sections 56 through 58 on the new creation.

If you are unable to locate a copy of this testimony, you may wish to substitute several questions from the Heidelberg Catechism (Q & A 26-27) or appropriate sections on creation and providence from other creeds and confessions. Also appropriate would be a hymn with this same theme, such as "How Great Thou Art."

■ **Focus 2:** *God*

Isaiah 40:12-31 is a sweeping and panoramic view of God, full of rich and diverse imagery that reveals God's grandeur. Ask the group to list all the qualities or attributes of God that this passage highlights. Next ask the group to describe God's relationship to his creation or to his kingdom.

Summarize by noting that God's kingly rule extends to every square inch of creation. This is the God who has no rival and who seeks to bring everything in creation under his rule and lordship.

■ **Focus 3:** *Today's Kingdom*

Using Timmer's material as background and encouraging participants to rely on Scripture and other sources, have them consider the questions below. To facilitate discussion, break the large group into smaller groups of three to five people each.

Ask the questions one at a time, allowing a brief time for small group discussion followed by a large group discussion with input from each of the small groups.

Q. In your experience, how much emphasis is given to the kingdom of God in today's Christianity?

Q. In your opinion, do most Christians relate their daily experiences to Christ's kingdom? Give examples to support your answer.

Q. What details of day-to-day living might look different in a kingdom-centered life?

■ Focus 4: *Three Short Parables*

Timmer concludes his discussion on the kingdom of God with a brief look at three rather short parables. Each of these parables provides a perspective on the appearance of the kingdom of God. Things are not always as they seem. Briefly review these parables with your group:

The *parable of the seed growing secretly* compares the work of God to the work of a farmer. Though it appears that the farmer is doing nothing, in time the hidden harvest will materialize.

So it is with God and his kingdom.

In the *parable of the mustard seed* the kingdom of God appears small and insignificant. But great things can be expected, particularly in the seemingly insignificant areas of life.

In the *parable of the yeast* a hidden and seemingly lost pinch of yeast produces a quiet change that overwhelms the dough. The Kingdom is sometimes like that yeast, gradually changing our perceptions until they are centered on the things of God.

Q. How do these parables shape our attitude toward the kingdom of God? (They provide us with encouragement, hope, and expectation, all characteristics of a kingdom-centered life.)

■ Focus 5: *Closing*

End this session with the previously mentioned reading from *Our World Belongs to God* and a brief prayer.

Conclude by asking group members to read chapter 3 of Timmer's book for the next session.

SESSION THREEE

The Jesus Parable

Introductory and Background Comments for the Leader

Jesus' parables focus on one significant and magnificent theme—*the kingdom of God.*

John the Baptist had preached that the kingdom was close and had urged people to prepare themselves for its arrival: "Repent, for *the kingdom of heaven* is near" (Matt. 3:1). When Jesus began his ministry, people noticed that he "went throughout Galilee, teaching in their synagogues and preaching *the good news of the kingdom* and healing every disease and sickness among the people" (Matt. 4:23).

The kingdom was not a new theme to those who heard John and Jesus. Those at the heart of Israel had long believed in the lordship of God and his kingly rule over his people. But their view of the kingdom was more heaven-centered than earth- realized. They waited for that day when God would establish his kingdom here on earth, and notions abounded as to how this kingdom would appear.

Then came John, and then came Jesus. With them came conflict for those who on the one hand sat in waiting for the kingdom but on the other hand never suspected for a moment that it would come as it did—heralded by a man who was the essence of the alternative life-style. John, a man who ate locusts and wild honey while sporting leather and camel's hair for clothing, was too much for the Jewish establishment. Both his appearance and his rhetoric created dissonance for the Jewish leaders.

What the people failed to realize was that here already was a clue to the secret of God's kingdom. For it was in the very disturbing nature of John that God was beginning to introduce his kingdom—a kingdom characterized by the unexpected, the shocking, the alternative.

John's presence set a tone for Jesus and his teaching that would eventually outstrip John's shock value among the Jewish mainliners. Upon Jesus' arrival, the questions only intensified: How could what he taught and revealed possibly be the stuff of which the kingdom of God was made?

Though recognizing the conflict his presence and movements were creating among members of the establishment, Jesus proceeded to teach both the disciples and others about the nature, the ways, and the character of God's kingdom. But note that Jesus appeared reluctant to "tell it like it is." He opted to tell people about the kingdom indirectly, on the angle, from a different slant.

And the response of those who heard Jesus? At one point Jesus' critics were so frustrated by his figurative and allusive style of teaching that they exclaimed, "How long will you keep us in suspense? If you are the Christ, tell us plainly." Jesus' response was simply, "I did tell you, but you do not believe" (John 10:24-25).

What was it that drove Jesus' ancient listeners to such frustration?

It was his telling of parables.

And what is it that confounds the modern reader of the parables?

Like the Pharisees, the members of your group are probably people who prefer straightforward information, rational theology, and lots of technical-sounding words. "Jesus," we are told in Matthew 13:34, "spoke all these things to the crowd in parables; he did not say anything to them without using a parable." These are disturbing words to anyone who prefers Jesus to be a little more like Paul when it comes to explaining things the way they are. But that is precisely what lies behind this "launching-pad" parable of Jesus, the parable of the sower.

The disciples asked Jesus why he used parables to describe the kingdom of God when a simple explanation would suffice. Jesus' response suggests that the kingdom is not something which is easily measured or defined or explained. Rather, understanding the kingdom of God takes great effort, because this kingdom is unlike anything we have known up to this point.

So Jesus explains the kingdom by connecting us with something we *do* know. As Timmer points out, Jesus, in his parables, connects the familiar with the unfamiliar. The kingdom is not "this" exactly, but "like" this. Therefore the use of metaphor. Therefore Jesus' use of parables.

Purpose of the Study

This session will lead the group to a new perspective not only on this particular parable but on parables in general. Participants will be encouraged to begin seeing the parables as metaphors.

In addition, group members will be asked to examine their faith in light of the soil samples given in the parable, perhaps moving them to shift their attitude towards the teaching of Jesus.

Note: Since this is the first major parable you will be discussing as a group and since it lays the groundwork for the other parables, you may want to spend two sessions discussing the material that follows.

■ Focus 1: *Hearing the Story*

Have the group arrange themselves in a circle. Ask participants to close their eyes as you or someone in your group delivers a dramatic telling (or a reading) of this parable. A possible beginning is as follows: "Imagine a spring day in Israel. It's early morning, and the land is still damp from the morning dew. You can begin to feel the heat of the morning sun. The farmer walks over to the shed where the seed is stored . . . ."

You may wish to incorporate a few of the following details into your story:

Detail 1: Explain that farmers in Palestine typically used one of two methods to scatter their seed. Either they flung a seed bag over their shoulder and scattered the seed by hand indiscriminately over the ground or they tied two bags over the shoulder of an animal, punched holes in both bags, and then walked the animal through the fields.

Detail 2: Tell the group that due to the absence of fences, fields were often unmarked and open to the free-wheeling travel patterns of people. Therefore, paths were formed over the land and were not turned up before planting.

Detail 3: Describe the rest of the terrain—the rocks, bushes, and thorns—and explain how the sun scorched the plants. Embellish the telling of the story, but do not add to it anything that would distract the listener from the essence of the parable.

Detail 4: Be sure to include in your telling of the story the four types of soil and the crops they produced.

■ Focus 2: *Focus of the Parable*

A metaphor draws a connection between two things—things familiar with things unfamiliar (see chapter 1 of Timmer's book).

Q. What are the points of connection in the parable of the sower? Where do you think the point of surprise comes in this parable?

Traditionally, commentators have noted that this parable describes the various responses of the soil to the seed. Each soil represents a different type of listener.

Timmer argues that, in fact, the emphasis of this parable is not so much on the soil and its receptivity as it is on the sower himself, who corresponds to Jesus and his rule, and on the seed, which is the good news. The accent is on what the sower does—namely, scatter seed about a varied landscape. The point of surprise or shock comes when we realize that the kingdom of God comes through Jesus scattering the gospel (the seed) which appears weak and vulnerable.

Q. The parable reveals that the seed is sown indiscriminately, with almost reckless abandon. What implications does that have for our understanding of how the gospel reaches people?

■ Focus 3: *Why Parables?*

The telling of this parable poses this question in the minds of the disciples: *Why did Jesus explain the kingdom through parables?* Participants should struggle with this question as well. (See comments in the introductory and background comments for this session.) Then give the group the opportunity to offer their opinion of what the secret of the kingdom is, using the parable of the sower as the basis for their response.

Some of the following comments may guide your discussion:

The secret of the kingdom appears to be centered in the question posed later by Jesus in Luke 9: "Who do people say that I am?" or "Who do you say that I am?" Our answer to this question determines the degree to which we understand the parables.

The kingdom has arrived in the person of Jesus. "It is in the midst of you," says Jesus at one point. So when Jesus speaks in parables, he is really drawing attention to the kingdom through himself. In the case of this parable, Jesus is regarded as the sower.

Unless we realize that Jesus is the key to understanding parables, the window through which we look to "perceive" or "see" the kingdom, we will be puzzled by these stories and their meanings. Recall that parables are metaphors that attempt to connect the familiar with the unfamiliar.

■ Focus 4: *Seeing the Kingdom's Growth*

On the basis of what Timmer suggests concerning the vulnerability of both the sower and the sowing in this parable and given what happened to the seed that falls on the first three soils, this parable may produce some doubts about the kingdom among members of your group. Raise the following two questions and discuss them together:

Q. Does the parable leave you feeling hope*less* or hope*ful* about the kingdom? Why?

Q. Mention some signs of the times that sometimes make you feel pessimistic about the kingdom's chances for gaining a foothold in this culture.

There is, in the end, a sense of something natural about the kingdom as there is about nature itself. Farming has its own hazards and disappointments, as any farmer is able to tell us. Growth and harvest are dependent on factors such a rain, sunshine, and heat. Yet, the farmer continues to believe that a harvest will be forthcoming. The God of the harvest is also the God of the rainfall and of the sunshine.

Likewise with the kingdom. There are great risks involved in spreading the Word, a Word that appears weak and vulnerable. The conditions that threaten the Word's effectiveness are numerous. However, Christians can remain confident that some of the seed will bear a reasonable if not surprising yield. God remains in control.

■ Focus 5: *Stages of Faith*

Timmer notes that the soils are different categories for viewing the various ways in which a person might respond to the seed, the Word. These categories are ways of describing the different circumstances surrounding the development of our own faith. We recognize that the life of faith is a growth process and that we pass through stages of faith much as we pass through stages of physical and social development.

Have the participants arrange themselves in groups of three or four persons. Ask these small groups to briefly discuss the following questions:

Q. Do you see evidence in your own life of times that you have shifted "categories" or stages in response to God or to the kingdom of God or to Jesus? You might describe a time when your faith was less productive, less active, and tell what God did to awaken or propel this faith into action.

Q. What does this change of soils suggest to you about faith? About God's ways of working in our lives? About the seed, the Word?

■ **Focus 6:** *Closing*

Timmer draws a conclusion from this parable: Not only is Jesus a teller of parables, but he is himself like a parable. Parables shock; Jesus shocks. Parables are often characterized by the unconventional; so is Jesus. Parables arrest our thoughts and tell us to rethink our ideas, to reorder our understanding of things; so does Jesus. In fact, he tells us not only to reorder but also to repent!

Jesus is God's parable. Has any greater parable ever been told?

Close your session by reflecting together on ways in which your discussion today has shifted or adjusted your view of God, the kingdom, Jesus, and this parable. Then offer a prayer of thanks to the Sower, the Lord of the harvest.

SESSION FOUR

The Hidden Treasure

A Quote for Reflection

> We guide by calling to mind men and women in whom the great vision becomes visible, people with whom we can identify, yet people who have broken out of the constraints of their time and place and moved into unknown fields with great courage and confidence. The rabbis guide their people with stories; ministers usually guide with ideas and theories.
>
> One of the remarkable qualities of the story is that it creates space. We can dwell in a story, walk around, find our place. The story confronts but does not oppress; the story inspires but does not manipulate. The story invites us to an encounter, a dialogue, a mutual sharing.
>
> A story that guides is a story that opens a door and offers us space in which to search and boundaries to help us find what we seek.
>
> Henri Nouwen,
> *The Living Reminder, pp. 65-66*

Introductory and Background Comments for the Leader

We might assert that few things last and few things are of ultimate value. And yet, we often pursue things and ideas we treasure as though they *are* of ultimate value and *will* last forever. Much of humanity has seemingly paid its pound of flesh for treasures that are as lasting as those who pursue them.

Jesus knows this about humanity.

He knows, we suspect, the things that make our hearts beat.

He knows those things which our imaginations fancy.

So Jesus gets our attention by talking about treasures—something he knows will capture our imaginations and cause our hearts to beat. Who has not read about treasures hidden in caves, buried under old floorboards, or tucked away in attic trunks? Tales of treasures catch our attention, making us wonder what it would be like to find such a trove. What would we do with a find that brought us great wealth and opportunity? Would such a find not draw us into the spotlight, make us instant celebrities and the envy of many?

Even in contemporary times we hear of lost treasures that are found and wonder to ourselves, "What if . . . ." To some degree, certainly, this is what a lottery does. Aside from the moral and ethical questions such a practice raises in our minds, we nevertheless find ourselves fantasizing about what we might do with that kind of money.

The things we treasure, however, go beyond the thoughts of silver and gold, money and precious jewels. We treasure or value many things for which we are willing to pay a high price. Often these are material things, but even ideas and relationships, values and ideologies are things on which we place significant value.

It is partly against this background that Jesus talks about the kingdom of God. Says Jesus on this and other occasions, "I want to talk to you about the kingdom of God. Now when you think about the kingdom, think of it like this. See if this helps you in your understanding." At this point he starts in on a story that catches our attention immediately because it includes the one thing we have all thought about at one time or another—treasures!

As Henri Nouwen suggests in the quote above, the story of the treasure invites us in, welcomes us to stay awhile and to find our place. Perhaps this story "will guide us out of the constraints of time and place and move us into unknown fields with great courage and confidence."

Purpose of this Study

After a reflective visit to this parable, participants will come to see that Jesus is asking people to evaluate their present life and to consider the life of the unknown kingdom. The parable sets a challenge before us—a challenge that appears to give something away for free, but actually exacts a price.

The group will be forced to reconsider what they value over against the values of God's kingdom.

■ Focus 1: *Hearing the Story*

As you did last week, ask group members to arrange their chairs in a circle, and to listen (perhaps with eyes closed) to a dramatic reading or telling of this parable. You may wish to ask a different member to present the parable each week.

■ Focus 2: *A Fable*

Read or tell the following Aesop fable to the group:

> A farmer who was about to die and wanted to familiarize his sons with his farm called them to him and said, "Boys, a treasure is buried in one of my vineyards."
>
> After he died, the sons took plows and mattocks (digging tools) and dug up their whole farm. They didn't find the treasure, but the vineyards repaid them with a much increased crop.

Q. Compare the parable of the hidden treasure to the Aesop story. What are its similarities and differences?

One key observation participants might make is that in Jesus' parable the man simply stumbles upon the treasure, while in Aesop's story the sons are looking for the hidden treasure. This same comparison could be made between the parable of the hidden treasure and the parable of the pearl that follows it in Matthew 13:45-46.

Q. What does the way in which the man found the treasure tell you about the nature of the kingdom of God?

The kingdom of God appears to have a holy freedom and a spontaneity about it, revealing itself in the routine of life. The kingdom can come ("your kingdom come . . .") anytime, anywhere. Though it is hidden in the routine of daily life, it has an element of surprise to it, cropping up where it will. So it is with grace.

■ Focus 3: *A Surprising Kingdom*

To bring home the point of how the kingdom of God sometimes comes to us in surprising ways, ask if any group members have experienced the surprise of the kingdom breaking into their lives at a time when they weren't looking for it. Invite one or two persons to briefly relate such a story to the group. (If possible, approach a few people earlier in the week—people who you know have been surprised in some way by the kingdom—and invite them to prepare a brief telling of their stories. Timmer's examples of Paul, the Ethiopian Eunuch, and Mary of Magdala might help you in finding such individuals.)

If no such story presents itself in your group, consider relating the following commentary and true story about Frank to the group.

Timmer highlights the story of the rich young ruler, perhaps the first yuppie. Jesus essentially asks the young man if it is possible for him to liquidate all of his assets, those things he values most, in order that he might pursue Jesus and the things of his kingdom. The tragedy in this story is that the rich young ruler turns his back on the treasure offered him by Jesus.

This is the thing we must come to grips with when hearing the parables of Jesus. Jesus' parables are more than interesting, entertaining, and thought-provoking. They are stories that are out to arrest our thinking and the ways of life we are so comfortable with. Timmer suggests that this parable is out to revolutionize our lives, to turn our values upside down.

Associating with Jesus is risky business.

Consider this story (or stories, if members of your group have experiences to share) of a young man, whom we'll call Frank.

A Story that Bears Witness to the Treasure Story

Frank was a fourth-year student at Stanford University who went on to graduate at the top of his class. While at Stanford, he served on a number of blue-ribbon committees and prestigious study groups. Even before graduation from Stanford, Frank received numerous graduate scholarship offers from leading schools around the country and was offered high-salaried positions with notable companies.

At the time all of this happened Frank was not a Christian, and up to this point in his life had shown little interest in so-called "spiritual" things. But one day, when Frank was out digging in the fields of academia, the blade of his mind came upon the treasure of Jesus. Poking around the Stanford Library, he came across the Bible. He turned to and read the Gospels (Matthew, Mark, Luke, and John). He was struck by the significance and immensity of the treasure he had encountered in the routine of his academic life. Whatever he had valued up this point, whatever he had been taught to value by this culture up to now, was beginning to shift.

Two months after his graduation Frank sold all that he had treasured, left behind the offers of scholarships and high salaried positions, and moved to another university town to take up the kingdom work there among students. Today he lives off a very meager income while pointing each generation of students to the treasured Jesus and his kingdom.

After listening to Frank's story and/or the stories of participants, discuss the following questions together:

Q. Some might claim that this story (or these stories) runs contrary to a saying of Jesus, "Seek and ye shall find." Perhaps "Do not seek and ye may find" would have been more appropriate. Ask the group which phrasing seems more accurate, based on the story and what they've learned about Jesus' parables and the nature of his kingdom.

The man in Jesus' parable was not looking for the kingdom.

Neither was Frank in our story.

And that's one of the ways the kingdom comes to us—by surprise. We are halted in our tracks, in our routine, and perhaps even in our indifference to life. The plow of our daily routine hits the hidden treasure of the kingdom, and we are jolted for a moment. In that moment we are faced with a decision: to sell or to hold on to those things we value so dearly.

Q. Do you believe that the kingdom is really so demanding that it would ask of us the very things we treasure most deeply? What things might you have to give up?

Q. What affect did finding the treasure have on the man in the parable?

■ Focus 4: *Radical Responses*

In the finding of the treasure, we discover that we are found. The parable locates us, finds us out. The man in the parable quickly comes to grips with the present state of his life and moves into action.

Likewise, when encountering the treasure we call the kingdom, we are forced to evaluate our own situation, our goals, and what we think is important. Invariably we are confronted with two choices: we will either walk away from the kingdom's costly demands or face up to its challenge and begin to sell off the lesser treasures of our lives.

As this brief parable seems to suggest, suddenly the finding of the kingdom opens up new possibilities, new adventures, new challenges. One is catapulted out of the routine and into a new reality called the kingdom.

The following story might help get at some of the dynamics involved when people make radical choices for the kingdom of God.

> A number of years back a couple from Colorado made a radical decision to sell many of the things that they had come to treasure. Though they had known the reality of God in their lives for a long time, they perceived that the kingdom was asking for something more. After the husband terminated his prestigious job with the city the couple liquidated most of their assets, said goodbye to their family and friends, and set out for Africa with a Christian world relief organization. They landed in a part of Africa riddled with civil strife, hunger, and disease but remained convicted that this calling was the thing they were to treasure over many of the things they had been encultured to treasure.
>
> The response of Christians and non-Christians alike to what this couple did was varied. Some affirmed them. Others wondered if they hadn't taken their Christian faith too far. Many, in the face of this couple's explanation as to why they were embarking on this adventure of faith, stood speechless. Even the local newspaper could not cover the story without mumbling something about the oddity of giving up so much for the unknown.

For this couple, however, the move to Africa meant catching the spirit of this parable in pursuing the things of God.

■ **Focus 5:** *Closing*

As you conclude your session, ask the group about their overall reaction to the parable of the hidden treasure.

Q. What implications might this parable have for your congregation? For each group participant personally?

Close with prayer, thanking God for the surprise of his kingdom and asking for his help in catching the spirit of the parable, in being willing to give up all for his kingdom.

SESSION FIVE

The Friend at Midnight

Introductory and Background Comments for the Leader

Each of us is a creature of culture. The culture we belong to shapes our values, hopes, and dreams and affects the way we live out the twenty-four-hour periods of our lives.

Our culture has so much impact on our understanding of reality that we sometimes have trouble understanding other cultures. What happens, for example, when something that is said or done in one culture is resaid or redone in another culture? Thom Hopler, in his book *A World of Difference*, relates a personal incident from his experience as a missionary to Kenya:

> "How much did you pay for your wife?" the old man asked during the first month Marcia and I spent in Kenya. When I explained that we don't sell women in America, he laughed and said, squeezing Marcia's thin arm, "I wouldn't give a goat for her either."

Hopler went on to say,

> People are different. Not only do individuals differ from one another, but groups of people differ as well. On another occasion in my first months in Africa, I waved hello to a friend across the street. Immediately he ran over to me asking,"What's the matter? What do you want?" I spent the next ten minutes trying to talk my way out of that innocent cultural misstep. My hand signal did not mean "Hello," but "Come here quickly. I need you."

As Hopler and many others like him have discovered, failure to understand a given culture can lead to misunderstandings about people and the things they are trying to communicate.

In this chapter, Timmer points out that we have traditionally misunderstood the parable of the friend at midnight because we have examined it through the eyes of our Western culture. To really understand what Jesus intended, we must take a new look at this parable in the context of the Middle Eastern culture in which it was first told.

Purpose of the Study

In this session participants will discover that understanding the cultural values surrounding this story will lead us to celebrate the profound goodness and dependability of God. The group will recognize the reliability of God in keeping his covenant promises. They will see the God who transcends culture and who draws all of us to live out values that are appropriate to kingdom living. Participants will also recognize the implications of hospitality as it is understood in the Middle East and perhaps as it should be understood by all those in God's kingdom.

■ Focus 1: *Hearing the Story*

Invite group members to gather in the circle and listen to today's presentation (read or told) of the parable.

■ Focus 2: *What the Parable Means*

Begin by asking members of the group to give brief explanations of how they have understood this parable up to now. In what context have they heard certain explanations of this parable (i.e., a sermon or discussion on prayer, a teaching on perseverance, or in another context)? Also ask for some brief reactions to Timmer's explanation of the parable. (Simply note the responses without elaborating on them. That will come later.)

As the discussion develops, try to lead participants to a richer view of the parable and the reality of God's goodness and reliability. But don't make them feel embarrassed about their previous understanding (or as Timmer points out, "misunderstanding") of the parable. It might be that some will still maintain that this parable has something to do with perseverance. Allow for difference of perspective while encouraging and affirming new insights.

■ Focus 3: *Can You Imagine?*

This parable of Jesus rotates on the notion of the unthinkable, the impossible. Jesus assumes that no one in his right mind could possibly believe a certain thing would happen.

"Can any of you imagine?" he asks.

His listeners respond, "No! I can't imagine that."

Examples of things *we* can't imagine might be as follows:

"Can you imagine asking your spouse to bring home some milk and bread only to have him/her bring home a quart of motor oil and a bail of hay?"

"Can you imagine opening a present from a friend and discovering that she has given you garbage?"

Q. Think of similar situations that you might have difficulty imagining.

It is in this context of "Which of you . . ." or "Can you imagine. . ." that Jesus tells the parable of the friend at midnight. Jesus poses the unthinkable, the hard to believe.

Q. What do you think? Do you think that the incident related by Jesus would be unthinkable in Western culture? What is it about the incident that strikes you as unthinkable? How might your neighbors respond if you were to call on them at midnight? How might you respond if someone came calling at midnight?

■ Focus 4: *Hospitality*

Explain that the village dwellers of Palestine took membership in their community very seriously where matters of hospitality were concerned. The person who received a visit from a journeying friend felt obligated to extend the finest in hospitality.

Q. Describe the attitude in our culture toward hospitality. Where and in what ways might the attitude described in the parable be appropriate and helpful in our society?

Q. What might this parable be telling you about your understanding of Christian community (the church) and the role of hospitality?

Be sure to briefly discuss the need for more hospitality in the Christian community. Refusing hospitality to others should be as unthinkable in the church as it was to those who first listened to Jesus' story.

■ Focus 5: *The Meaning of* Anadeia

Have the group divide into smaller groups of three to five people to discuss the three questions stated below. Discussion should run about four or five minutes per question. Explain that after making various cultural observations regarding the setting of this parable, Timmer organizes his discussion on the meaning of this parable around the Greek word *anadeia.* Timmer points out the different meanings of the word and then applies those meanings to the actual text. Have the small groups discuss briefly the three alternatives Timmer suggests as possible interpretations of *anadeia.*

First comes the suggestion that the host is shameless.

Q. Based on what the author suggests and your own thinking, does he draw the right conclusion about the shamelessness of the host? In drawing the parallel, raise Timmer's question—namely, "Is it shameless for the believer to take his or her request to God in prayer?"

The second alternative centers on the possibility that the host is viewed as a persistent fellow. This is perhaps the most widely held view of the meaning of the word *anadeia* and therefore also of the parable overall. In this discussion, Timmer argues that we must stay within what the text actually says.

Q. What does the text say about persistence?

Thirdly, Timmer turns our attention to yet another meaning of *anadeia,* the one that perhaps provides a new twist to our understanding of the text. Arguing that the wording of the text and the cultural norms of the day do not permit a reading of the host as shameless, Timmer makes a case for the shamelessness of the sleeping neighbor.

Q. Evaluate Timmer's argument. Do you find it reasonable and helpful? Unreasonable and unhelpful? Defend your position.

■ Focus 6: *The Parable and Us*

Have the small groups remain together as you talk about the implications of this parable for us.

Q. What does this parable mean for our understanding of God, the King of the kingdom?

The story characterizes God as a King who is not arbitrary, but faithful. He keeps his Word.

We can trust him to listen to us at any time because he is, we might say, the great insomniac who "will neither slumber nor sleep" (Ps. 121:4).

However, even here we experience a shift in culture and to many twentieth-century Westerners, God seems very far away. The episodes we read in the Bible belong to another time and place; almost, it might be argued, in another world. We are spectators looking into a culture about which we know very little. We are foreigners.

Q. We believe that the things of which Jesus speaks were true of how God *once* interacted with people, but what bearing does that have on our relationship with him today?

After the groups have discussed this question for a few minutes, conclude together that perhaps we do not seek or expect the degree of intimacy with God that people had back there—in *that* culture. "That was then and this is now," we might exclaim. We overcome the problem of time and place, in part, by recognizing the role of God through the ages: he stays the same; he remains vital. As Hebrews 13:8 tells us, "He is the same yesterday, today and forever." In the passing of time, God's aim and principles of interaction with humanity remain consistent. He refuses to act out of character.

■ **Focus 7:** *Closing*

Q. How has your view of the parable changed through this discussion? Your view of the character of God?

Q. How does this parable help shape your views on coming to God in prayer?

Close by asking each participant to pray silently, using the following sentence as a guide: "One thing I commit myself to in the light of this parable is . . ."

SESSION SIX

The Suffering Father

Introductory and Background Comments for the Leader

Helmut Thielicke, author of *The Waiting Father,* provides a helpful comment for approaching and understanding this parable. He suggests that the parable is a sort of invitation to stand in the shoes of those who came near to Jesus. We are to look upon Jesus from their vantage point. Then, as the story unfolds, it begins to turn. It is in the turning of the story that we at some point declare, "This is me!" We recognize that Jesus is talking about us. We begin to identify with either of the two sons, depending on where we come from.

In the face of the father, we begin to see *the Father.* We begin to understand that here is a picture of God as he is and always has been. Here is not a god who can be relativized to fit our own limited theologies, a god we can fashion into our own image. Here is the God of Scripture, the God of ages past, and the God of contemporary humanity.

This is a mirror parable, a parable into which we gaze with squinting effort. It's as though we have walked into a steamy bathroom, and the mirror is all fogged up. But as the misty residue on the mirror begins to evaporate, the unclear becomes clear, and we are faced with the reality of ourselves and of our own predicament.

Purpose of the Study

Participants will come to identify with the experience of either or both brothers in this story. They will be asked to recall their own experience in relating to God the Father and to describe how that experience has shaped their response to God's love.

Group members will also have to make some decisions about their attitude toward those who appear distant from the kingdom but who nevertheless need to experience God's mercy.

■ Focus 1: *Hearing the Story*

Once again, ask the group to gather in a circle and prepare to listen to today's presentation (read or told) of the parable.

■ **Focus 2:** *Freedom*

As a general opening discussion, have the students simply relate some of the impressions that Timmer's comments made on them as they read through the chapter on the parable of the suffering father. Then focus on the struggle between the father and his youngest son.

Point out that the confrontation in the first portion of this parable is between a father and his child. The child is perhaps stumbling somewhere in the vast and misty terrain of adolescence. He's trying to find himself, and in his pursuit, he believes that the issue is his freedom. Tired of the constraints of home life, fed up with the dos and don'ts of living under his father's roof, he looks out on the world and imagines a better life. Out there is a life unbounded by the rules of his father: days and nights of adventurous living where weekdays and weekends run together as one.

Q. Think back to your own childhood, in particular those years of change between twelve and twenty. In what ways do the younger son's attitude and thinking remind you of some of your own experiences as a teenager?

James Fowler, author of *Stages of Faith* argues rather convincingly that as we develop and grow physically and cognitively, so too we develop spiritually, passing through different stages of faith.

Q. At what stage in our faith development do you suspect we might pass through a more critical and sometimes rebellious phase? What value might there be in a period of raging against and shaking a fist in God's face, perhaps even turning one's back on God and heading for the open spaces?

Q. How might the church make more adequate room for the role of doubts and questions in one's faith formation? For example, should the church periodically sponsor a class for doubters and skeptics?

Q. How should the Christian community respond to those who appear to have left "home" for the freedom of the open spaces?

In connection with this discussion, Timmer relates Kierkegaard's story of the lily. Tying the story together with the parable, Timmer observes that "freedom is dependence upon the father" and "freedom is a son at home with the father."

Q. How would you explain this sense of freedom to a teenager or to any person struggling with the whole notion of freedom and independence?

■ Focus 3: *The Father*

Focus your discussion now on the father, encouraging participants to try to see the events of the story through his eyes. Note that the father puts up no defense, no reaction to his son's behavior. He quietly lets the son go, without protest, without any evidence of arguing that it would be best for the son to stay at home.

Q. Imagine what the father felt like as he stood at the door, watching his son leave home. Describe the look on his face and then the thoughts behind those looks.

Once we acknowledge the deep offense and humiliation the son caused by demanding his inheritance and leaving home, the father's reaction when his son returns becomes even more remarkable. Timmer acquaints us with the custom of the day as it applies to both the estranged son and to the father, and points out that the father rushes out, ignoring custom. In the face of a tradition in which everything is done decently and in good order, this father, in a spurt of joy and forgiveness, runs out to greet his son. He does this at great cost to himself—the cost of humility, the cost of many who will wag their tongues in criticism of the father's defiance of social standards.

This picture of the father is really a picture of the King of the kingdom. From the Pharisee's perspective, this was no way for the King, for God, to act. How dare God disregard the rules of tradition?

Point out that many of us, too, have inherited or bought into a tradition of being able to see God only in certain ways, in certain places, and at certain times.

Q. How might we break out of our stereotypical thinking about God?

■ Focus 4: *Grace Versus Moralism*

Jesus presents the Father of heaven as the God of the unexpected, the God who catches us off guard and turns our way of thinking upside down. Our sometimes arrogant view of the gospel holds that the kingdom is a rather exclusive club for the elite. In order to join, one has to first jump the hurdles of law and right living. The moralist side of us insists that people meet the requirements imposed upon us by ceremony and tradition.

Jesus sees this barricade between sinners and the kingdom and hastens to blast it away with his parables. This parable blasts through the moralistic barricades erected outside the kingdom by offering this picture: a father waiting at the end of a long lane day after day until he sees the figure of a wayward child returning home. The child is stooped over from the weight of his sin coupled by the weight of the laws that he is told to keep. The father moves out toward the sinner in the spirit of Jesus' words: "My yoke is easy and my burden is light" (Matt. 11:30). The father throws his arms around the child, hugs and holds him, and takes from him the burdens of sin and the law's demands that he cannot meet. He then clothes his child in the cloak of salvation—free, without charge.

Q. How should this picture shape our views on those who appear so distant from the kingdom? On outreach?

Q. In what ways might your church reflect the spirit of this parable in the attitude it presents toward "sinners"? In what ways might your congregation be communicating exclusiveness to those who are looking for a church home?

■ Focus 5: *The Older Son*

Timmer appropriately entitles this parable "The Suffering Father." Evidence of that suffering is provided in the initial break of the relationship between the younger son and the father. How his older son responded to his treatment of the younger son must have broken the father's heart.

Clarence Jordan, in *Cotton Patch Parables of Liberation* says this in connection with the older son's response:

> Jesus is delivering this hard parable to us not as a last word of utter condemnation, but as a final appeal to us to abandon our elder-brother role, our self-assurance, our apathy, our possessiveness, our casual "obedience".

In the words of Timmer, the older brother's role "is to greet the guests and make sure everyone has enough to eat and drink."

Q. How would you translate this behavior into contemporary terms? What would you need in order to live out the spirit of this custom?

■ Focus 6: *Gentiles and Jews*

The older son is left outside in the dark. The older son, asserts Timmer, represents Israel.

The younger son is inside, enjoying the light, enjoying the feast. The younger son represents the Gentile nations.

And where is the father? He is outside pleading with the older son to come into the light, to sit at the banquet table with the younger son. God is pleading with Israel, the older son, to come inside but Israel refuses. Israel refuses to accept Jesus as the Messiah.

Q. If we are the younger sons and daughters of God the Father, and we have eaten at his table, where are we to be found? In other words, are we called to suffer with God, to go out in the darkness where the older brother lingers, or are we called simply to enjoy the festivities inside?

Q. How might this story end?

■ **Focus 7:** *Closing*

End this session in a time of quiet reflection and prayer, using the following words as an entry into this time: "Oh suffering Father, receive these thoughts with your open and waiting arms . . . ."

SESSION SEVEN

The Messianic Banquet

Introductory and Background Comments for the Leader

It might prove helpful to remind ourselves of what Jesus is up to in telling these parables. Perhaps this story will position our thinking (and your group's, if you choose to read or tell it to them).

> There once was a navy officer who dreamed of someday commanding one of the navy's finest ships. Finally his dream became a reality. He was given a commission to serve on one of the newest and proudest ships in the fleet.
>
> One stormy night, while the ship was plowing through the sea, the captain was on bridge. Suddenly, off to port side he spotted a strange light rapidly approaching. He quickly ordered his signalman to flash a message to this oncoming craft: "Alter your course 10 degrees to the south."
>
> A moment passed before the reply came: "Alter your course 10 degrees to the north."
>
> Determined that his ship would take a back seat to none, the captain snapped back the order, "Alter your course 10 degrees—I am the Captain."
>
> The response beamed back, "Alter your course 10 degrees—I am Seaman Third Class Jones."
>
> Now infuriated, the Captain grabbed the signal light with his own hands and fired off the message, "Alter your course. I am a battleship."
>
> The reply came back, "Alter your course. I am a lighthouse."

This humorous though poignant story illustrates the fact that regardless of how big any of us might be, God's Word stands as an unchanging beacon in our lives. All other courses must be altered to his course or shipwrecks are inevitable.

In the parables, Jesus calls to his listeners, urging them to alter their course, to change their understanding, their perception, of the kingdom and its king. "And though the kingdom is not precisely 'this' it is certainly 'like this,'" Jesus tells us. And because it is "like this," we should respond appropriately by altering our course.

Of particular interest to our understanding of the parable of the banquet feast is the social structure of Jesus' day. As in our day, society in Jesus' day fell prey to a pecking order. Simply stated, those with power and prestige were at the top while those who were poor and dispossessed were at the bottom. Here, too, was a culture of the haves and the have-nots, in which those who had power made sure that those who had no power never got it.

Jesus confronted this pecking order and the arrogance that accompanied it head on in this parable.

Purpose of the Study

In this study, participants will meet the host of the messianic banquet, a host who will not permit his plans to be stopped and whose guest list includes a few surprises for those who are receptive to his invitation.

■ **Focus 1:** *Hearing the Story*

Again, open your session by having a group member read or tell today's parable. Since Timmer's discussion is based primarily on the account in Luke 14:16-24, that passage would be most appropriate for class presentation.

■ **Focus 2:** *A Look at Our Culture*

'In order to make this parable more relevant to our thinking, it may be helpful to analyze the social dynamics of our own culture.

Q. Who, in our culture, are the poor, the lepers, the oppressed women, the diseased, the "least of these" to whom Jesus often referred in his teaching? Who are the powerful, the prestigious?

After you've focused briefly on our culture in general, encourage the group to paint a brief picture of the social makeup of your church and the community in which the church is located.

Q. Does the church reflect the social stratification of the surrounding community? What kind of people does the church attract? What groups from around the church community are left out of the church body?

It is this kind of preparatory work that will place the parable in more dramatic relief.

■ Focus 3: *The Kingdom*

Remind the group that as we noted in the introduction to the study of Jesus' parables (chapters 1 & 2) and again at the outset of this session, Jesus was attempting to describe the character of God's kingdom. In effect, Jesus is here saying, "The kingdom of God is like a feast to which some were invited and did not come, to which others were invited and did come, and to which some are still coming."

Take a few minutes with the group, trying to put the parable into today's language. What Jesus is suggesting is that the kingdom is like a big party to which *all kinds* of people are invited. There is plenty of food and drink, and music charges the air. A spirit of joy and festivity pervades the occasion. Use the following questions to focus your discussion:

Q. Describe the setting and atmosphere of this feast as you take time to imagine it in your mind. What images spring to mind when someone says to you, "You are invited to a party"? How does that human invitation compare with the invitation to attend a party hosted by God?

As you discuss this metaphor together, point out that while we may be startled by the comparison Jesus makes between the kingdom and a party, it's likely that Jesus' listeners were not. Because the Old Testament made many references to a great feast, the Jews of Jesus' day believed that the dawning of the messianic age would culminate in a feast of great proportion. So Jesus stood on solid ground in telling this parable.

Ask group members to close their eyes briefly and to relax as they consider the following questions:

Q. What do you suppose was running through Jesus' mind as he drew attention to the kingdom as a feast, a party? Does Jesus' choice of metaphor square with other things Jesus' teachings reveal about the kingdom of God?

Point out that the choice of a party as a metaphor gives us insight into how Jesus views the kingdom. He sees it not as a dull, boring place, burdened with rules and regulations, but as a bright, joyful celebration.

Q. Is your perception of God's kingdom shifting at all? Can you describe this shift?

Explain that perhaps this is where Jesus' humanity and divinity come into crisp focus. Here Jesus has one eye firmly fixed on the divine future in the presence of God as the other eye catches a glimpse of an earthly party bathed in hilarity and joy. Jesus is using the metaphor of a familiar feast as an invitation into fellowship with God.

Q. If your church were to preach and live out a "feast theology," how might people view the kingdom, and thus Christianity, differently?

Imagine together what people might say of your church: "Now there is a church that knows how to celebrate life! There is a church caught up in joy and festive fussing over other people! There is a church that worships God by calling other people to join them in the feast!"

To conclude your discussion, read Isaiah 55: 1 and consider how well your congregation communicates such an invitation to the community.

■ Focus 4: ***Excuses, Excuses!***

Timmer insightfully exposes the excuses given by the would-be guests for what they are—lies. Humanity's deceit and cover-up extend to the most horrifying extreme: turning down a divine invitation to join God for supper by telling a lie. Shades of Eden.

What is even more striking upon further reflection is the role of God. He is the initiator once again, and his initiation takes the form of a single word—come. Come as you are. This is the character of the King of the kingdom.

Q: Consider the types of folks Jesus invites to the feast. What qualifications does he look for in those who receive invitations? How do Jesus' standards for welcoming newcomers compare to the standards of your church and denomination?

■ Focus 5: ***The Host Responds***

Talk together about some of the options the host in Jesus' parable faced. How might Jesus' listeners have expected the parable to end? Point out how astonished they must have been when the "good" people turned down God's invitation. Those who had their theology "straight" headed for other priorities —cows, fields, and spouses.

Any human host would be faced with a number of choices at this point. It would be understandable if he spun off in a rage over the utter rudeness of those who were invited. We certainly wouldn't be surprised if he just sat and pouted over the seeming rejection of the invited guests. And we'd almost expect him to cancel the whole affair.

But the host in Jesus' parable is no human host.

Focus the next part of your discussion together on the very unexpected response of the host.

Q. How does the host respond? How might you respond under similar circumstances?

The host truly does surprise us. In fact, he appears to revel in his surprise. The hair-splitting dogmatists and the arrogant traditionalists walk away from the feast. Going into the feast are God's surprises—the poor, the "sinners," the hoodlums, the unlovable, the broken, all making their way inside to sit at the banquet table of the Lord.

Here too is a picture of the waiting Father, who is now also the inviting Father.

Q. What do you make of the guest list Jesus has drawn up for the feast?

Q. What is your personal response to Jesus' invitation? What is your attitude toward the others who will be seated next to you?

Q. What can you do to draw others into the feast, particularly those who might be outside your community?

■ **Focus 6:** *Closing*

In the final analysis, this is a parable more about the host, about God the Father, than it is about us, the guests.

Consider reading the passage from Isaiah 25:6-9 before asking the last question and inviting people to pray.

Q. What aspect of God's character comes through to you from this parable and the Isaiah text?

Closing Prayer: "God of the Feast, I have heard your invitation and I say in response . . . ."

SESSION EIGHT

The Rich Man and Lazarus

Introductory and Background Comments for the Leader

In Luke 16:16 Jesus says, "The Law and the Prophets were proclaimed until John; since that time the good news of the kingdom of God is being preached, and every one is forcing his way into it." He implies that his coming ushers in a new era in which people will have to face up to their old ways, their hollow traditions, their cultural biases, their relationships to people and things. Jesus comes on the scene and says, in effect, "Let go. These things will not satisfy. These things will lead to your destruction."

The new life to which Jesus calls people is costly. It demands that we ease our grip on things that either compete with or are substituted for the lordship of Christ in our lives. All who enter the kingdom must let go of the things they treasure more than the kingdom itself. This transformation can be violent: it involves a radical release of values, relationships and goods that interfere with the new things of God's kingdom.

However, leaving behind the old ways does not mean ignoring God's law. In Luke 16:17 we read, "It is easier for heaven and earth to disappear than for the least stroke of a pen to drop out of the Law." The laws of Moses and the words of the prophets still stand. They are now to be read in the context of God's kingdom. In no way are they to be ignored.

In particular, Jesus is out to confront the skepticism of the Pharisees regarding their notions about wealth and the kingdom. The Pharisees believed that wealth was evidence of God's favor upon them. Poverty was thus a sign of God's curse. This same attitude prevails in our own day as some voices peddle the doctrine of "Divine Prosperity." Statements such as, "God doesn't want Satan and his bunch to have all the diamonds. The King's kids get some too" are typical of this viewpoint.

In this parable Jesus is out to confront this perspective on wealth and pleasure-seeking. In effect, Jesus is warning those who view wealth falsely, "Keep up that kind of thinking and you'll end up in the same predicament as the rich man."

Because Jesus has no home, no bank account, no visible means of support, his very life-style draws attention to the issues he raises in this parable.

Purpose of this Study

This study will lead participants to examine their views on money and wealth in the context of biblical teaching and to reevaluate their attitude toward justice for the poor.

■ **Focus 1:** ***Hearing the Story***

After the group has gathered in a circle, ask today's presenter to read or tell the parable of the rich man and Lazarus.

■ **Focus 2:** ***The Reversal***

Jesus' parables are often shouts of reversal. As the story unfolds, the listener is presented with the way things are and then the way things are is turned upside down.

In this parable, Jesus points to the reality of the haves and the have-nots and indicates that the haves seem little interested in the plight of the have-nots. Then suddenly Jesus turns everything upside down: the haves *become* the have-nots.

To help the group appreciate the drama of the reversal in this parable, note that Jesus' story can be viewed as a three-act play. Ask participants to briefly summarize each of the three acts. (If you have time, you may even want to have the group quickly dramatize the three acts.)

Q. Compare the status of the two main characters in each of the three acts. Where does the reversal take place?

Q. What did this parable teach Jesus' listeners about the here and now? What does it teach us?

■ **Focus 3:** *The Context*

Timmer sees this parable in the context of the love of money. As you talk about that context with the group, point out that it might be said that the Western church preaches Jesus, but just enough Jesus to permit Christians to still be comfortable with the things of this culture.

Q. What do you suppose this statement means?

Perhaps we ought to consider having just enough Jesus to make us *un*comfortable with this culture. Jesus was a practical as well as theoretical teacher. On more than one occasion he put money and the kingdom into perspective for his listeners. Jesus' thesis was this: "No servant can serve two masters; either he will hate the one and love the other, or he will be devoted to the one and despise the other. You cannot serve both God and Money" (Luke 16:13).

The Pharisees were perceived as lovers of money. This parable is Jesus' warning to the Pharisees about the dangers of what they love.

Q. Is money the issue here? If so, what are Jesus' views on money based on this and other texts that contain his teachings? How do these views on money and wealth fit in with your views?

Q. Evaluate the life-style of North American Christians. In what ways do their economic views and life-style differ from those in the surrounding culture? Can you point to anything particularly Christian or biblical in the life-styles of members of your congregation? In your own life-style?

■ **Focus 4:** *An Experiment*

Timmer suggests that this parable has to do with seeing, or perhaps a lack of seeing. Jesus had commented earlier, in connection with parable-telling, that some "may be ever seeing but never perceiving, and ever hearing but never understanding" (Mark 4:12).

As he tells the parable, suggests Timmer, Jesus is trying to teach people to see things from God's perspective, to see people the way God sees them. The parable serves as a spotlight, if not a floodlight, on those in need.

Q. In the parable the spotlight is on the needy Lazarus. If Jesus were telling the parable today—perhaps to your congregation—who might the spotlight be on?

■ **Focus 5:** *Moses and the Prophets*

Remind the group that Timmer goes on to suggest that in the light of Moses and the prophets we can better see not only Lazarus but also those in need in our own times.

The things to which Moses and the prophets called our attention remain the things that ought to shape our kingdom perspective. They are parts of the kingdom equation.

The law of God is like a counselor directing us to holiness in the details of life. More often then not, we experience what might be called a "sanctification gap". Though we call ourselves Christians, we do not necessarily think or live Christianly. God's law calls us to live out our faith and respond to God's law in the details of everyday life.

What motivates us to live holy lives? Gratitude for what God has done for us. Like Israel, we remember our Egypt, our enslavement to sin, our pursuit of the things of this world. God's grace came and fetched us while we were yet sinners, slaves to our pride-ridden choices. In thankfulness to God's grace, we live out our lives with compassion, seeking after justice.

Q. Respond to this statement: "It is possible to be a Christian, yet not think or act like a Christian."

Q. What does this statement have to do with the parable of Lazarus and the rich man?

■ **Focus 6:** *God's Moral Law*

Remind the group of Timmer's assertion that prophets interpret current events in the light of God's moral will and call people to revive their covenant obligations through obedience to this law. Jesus is suggesting that we know what is demanded of us. We have access to God's moral law and need no further testimony from one who has returned from the dead.

Talk together about the rich man's plea, Abraham's response, and what Jesus is teaching through this part of the parable. The rich man pleads for personal mercy, but gets none. He's had his chance. He then appeals for mercy for his brothers by asking that someone warn them of their plight.

Q. How does Abraham respond to the rich man's request? Why? How might you respond to the rich man if he appealed to you personally? Would you be inclined to give him another chance?

This teaching of Jesus relates in part to the proper understanding of faith. The faith of the Pharisees demands a sign. At this point it ceases to be faith. "Signs" do not redeem. When we respond obediently to God's Word without further appeal for a sign, then we have what might be called "biblical faith."

In one sense of the word, *discipleship* involves a trust or a faith in God that rises above one's circumstances. For example, Christians who enjoy wealth and prosperity take little credit for earning them. And Christians who are immersed in pain and suffering still trust God to show himself in the midst of this suffering. Regardless of circumstance, we are asked to believe God, to take him at his Word, to live our lives dependently.

■ **Focus 7:** *Closing*

Q. There is a warning in this parable. What is it? How will you choose to respond in the face of it?

Q. What concrete steps might you take to demonstrate that you know God's ways and choose to follow them?

Close the session with a time of personal prayer, asking each participant to silently complete the following pledge: "I hear the teaching of Jesus, and I commit myself to . . . ."

SESSION NINE

The Compassionate Samaritan

Introductory and Background Comments for the Leader

It has been said more than once that "familiarity breeds contempt."

Our contempt may become evident, then, when we have to hear once again a familiar parable like that of the good Samaritan. Is there any parable that has been told and heard more often? There is hardly a preacher or teacher or youth leader that has not told this story repeatedly. And its telling and retelling has left people increasingly, though quietly, indifferent to its message. This contempt is due in part to the way people typically use the parable. Speakers suggest that the parable's message is, "Be kind to your neighbor; be a good Samaritan; be a good guy." When reduced to an example of what it means to be a good neighbor, the parable of the good Samaritan loses its potency. This is not to suggest that this is an unacceptable interpretation of the parable. There is much to support this meaning. But we should examine other perspectives on this familiar parable, such as those provided by Timmer's thoughtful reflections. These perspectives will enhance one's appreciation of the parable and thereby break the cycle of contempt created by its over-familiarity.

Recall again that parables locate the listener, strike a familiar chord in the listener's ear, and connect that familiarity with something less familiar in the kingdom. That is the function of a parable as metaphor.

A brief comment about hearing and seeing: From a certain vantage point, a person can see or hear things in a helpful and refreshing way. For instance, following a well-trodden path to the top of a hill or a mountain gives a person one perspective on the surrounding area. But leave the familiar path and venture out on a new approach to the summit of a mountain and the same person will see the surroundings from a different perspective. The author's commentary on this familiar parable provides this same kind of a different vantage point from which to "see" and "hear" the story of the Good Samaritan.

Purpose of this Study

Participants will be "led up the side" of this parable to two different vantage points: that of the Jewish listener and that of the priest in the parable. Readers will come to identify with one or both vantage points and will then select an appropriate response.

■ Focus 1: *Hearing the Story*

Ask today's presenter to tell or read this well-known parable.

■ Focus 2: *Identifying with the Listeners or the Characters*

Timmer asks readers first to assume the vantage point of a Jewish person who might be listening to this parable. The Jewish listener identifies with the person traveling this dangerous road. Many people he or she knows travel between Jerusalem and Jericho.

To heighten the group's identification with the Jewish traveler, remind them of an equally dangerous travel route in twentieth-century North America. Perhaps one possibility might be the route the college student takes at night between the library or lab and the dorm. Many assaults have occurred on university campuses at night.

Ask the group to imagine how they might react to a story about a woman who makes the decision to cross a darkened campus, even though assaults have occurred repeatedly there during the last few months. Discuss how they might be rightfully outraged and horrified by the crime but also a little critical of the woman's judgment: "What did she expect walking that dangerous route at night?" Then pose the following question:

Q. What similarities do you see between your response to the assault account and the response of Jesus' audience to the story of the traveler who was attacked on the Jericho road?

Explain that Jesus tells the parable in this way precisely because he wants to draw the people in. He wants them to identify with the victim who now lies beaten by the side of the road. This part of the story makes sense because the listeners can relate to its plausibility: "Yes, people *do* walk that road alone, but it certainly isn't a smart thing to do."

Once he draws his listeners in, they are eager to hear the outcome. They can imagine that *they* are lying beaten by the road, and they want to hear what happens. So much for scene I.

Remind the group of what takes place in scenes II and III. first a priest and then a Levite approach the victim on the road.

Q. What do you suppose Jesus' audience expected the priest to do? The Levite?

Q. Again, to put the story into today's terms, imagine that a minister is approaching the assault victim. What would *you* expect him to do?

■ Focus 3: *An Unexpected Twist*

As Timmer explains, the fourth scene contains a real shock, an unexpected twist. Jesus' listeners anticipate that a fellow-Jew, a layperson, will come along next to aid the Jewish victim. Instead, coming into view over the hump in the road is a "God-forsaken" Samaritan. It is this Samaritan who causes Jesus' audience to gasp! Considered a halfbreed by any "self-respecting" Jew, a Samaritan would not only be expected but also encouraged to keep moving down the road, to keep his hands off the Jew in the ditch.

The Jewish audience had been lying in the ditch, victimized. Then Jesus introduced the hero—the despised Samaritan.

Q. Again think in contemporary terms. Who might the despised Samaritan be in the assault story or in our society in general? How would you react to such a twist?

Jesus obviously intended his listeners—and that includes us—to identify with the helpless, beaten man in the ditch.

Q. Keeping that in mind, what does the parable say to us about the nature of God's mercy? Might God, in the person of Jesus, be our "Samaritan"? Explain.

■ Focus 4: *Restrictive Theology*

God's grace has picked us up out of our respective ditches. To paraphrase, "While we were yet helpless, God came to us in Jesus." Timmer now asks us to change perspectives, to change places. We move from the vantage point of the ditch to that of the road where we're asked to identify with the priest.

Often the crises of life test our theology and make it show its true face. Theology can either liberate its adherents or it can stifle and enslave those who claim to believe it.

Timmer retells the story of "The Unseemly Old Lady." It is a "before and after" kind of story. For the sake of discussion, have the group break into smaller groups of three to five people.

Q. What specific experiences in your life does this story remind you of—times or situations that set you free from your "old legalistic ways"?

Timmer draws a parallel between the behavior of the woman in the story and the behavior of the priest. He suggests that the priest is a victim of his theology. Perhaps, then, there are three victims in this story—the one beaten by the thieves and the two who were "beaten" by their theology.

Q. Think of some specific ways in which *our* theology might be enslaving us rather than liberating us.

■ Focus 5: *Working for Change*

Toward the end of his study on this parable, Timmer provides a poignant set of contemporary stories that find their parallel in the story of the good Samaritan. These stories serve to illustrate how deeply the theology of "walking on the other side" is ingrained in humanity.

Q. What elements of our theology and sociology might make it easy for us to "walk on the other side" rather than devote our time, energy, and money to helping victims of hunger, crime, abortion, discrimination, AIDS, and so on?

Q. How are our decisions in such situations affected by our race or ethical group? Our socio-economic status? Our culture? Our religion?

Q. How can we, as congregations and individuals, break out of the rules, traditions, and circumstances that keep us from fulfilling Jesus' law of love for our neighbor?

Q. Think of some concrete ways in which your congregation can begin "seeing" the need in the community around you and working for change.

■ Focus 6: *Closing*

This parable is *personal.* It attempts to create a sense of solidarity with one or another of the characters in the story. It first calls us to identify with the one beaten and lying at the side of the road. It then shifts our identification from the victim to that of the priest or Levite.

This parable is also *prophetic*. It warns us about our possible enslavement to a theology that keeps others enslaved or victimized by our refusal to care and to love.

This parable is also a call to *change,* to action. It pleads with us to recognize our solidarity with the one "saved" at the side of the road. It then asks us to reverse our perspective and calls us to care for others in need in the spirit of the One who ministered to us.

Ask the group to close by praying silently, thanking God for what they've learned in this parable and asking him to help them break out of the bonds of tradition that keep them from obedience. Or, offer the following petition, asking each group member to complete it silently:

"Jesus, in the form of the Samaritan, as you stooped down to bind my wounds, so will I . . . ."

SESSION TEN

The Shrewd Manager

Introductory and Background Comments for the Leader

The parable of the unjust steward poses many problems for the reader. Timmer highlights and addresses two of them.

It will be to your advantage as leader to spend extra time understanding the dynamics involved in this controversial parable and the three "sermon notes" that follow it.

The controversy that surrounds this parable appears on the surface to arise from the fact that Jesus seems to be applauding the questionable behavior of the unjust steward. Is Jesus in fact compromising with evil?

Below the surface, however, lies another possible source of irritation—namely, our attitudes toward money. The topic of money is a sensitive one for Christians, especially for those in affluent North America. Our growing privitization of life and faith coupled with our growing affluence makes any discussion of money and wealth a delicate one.

As a result, this parable might well provoke the students to raise issues that are peripheral to the thrust of this parable. That's not necessarily bad. If a fruitful discussion appears to be in the making, it might be advisable to let it run its course for a while. Depending on the direction this conversation takes, it will prove most helpful for you as leader to bring the group back to the parable at a point where the questions below touch on the group discussion.

Jesus' words are often confrontational. They sometimes alienate the listener at the point where he/she is most vulnerable. However, the lordship of Jesus Christ is all-encompassing and draws into its domain every aspect of one's life, including the matter of money. If Jesus appears to be stepping on toes, it must be because he is addressing issues that hit close to home. You are encouraged as leader to keep the discussion from turning angry or malicious, always promoting honesty and charity in potentially heated discussions.

The materials that follow suggest that you consider having your group dramatize the parable. Preparing a drama will take extra time and advance work but should prove to be helpful.

Purpose of this Study

The group will have an opportunity to work through some of the major "problems" or questions this parable presents. Participants will also gain a sense of the crisis with which believers are confronted in their journey of faith and will acknowledge Jesus' call to be resourceful in the face of such a crisis.

■ **Focus 1:** *Hearing the Story*

Invite today's presenter to read or tell the parable to the group.

■ **Focus 2:** *The Parable's Conclusion*

Timmer begins by addressing the problem of where, exactly, this parable ends. He makes a case for favoring the ending that incorporates verse 8a.

Q. Are you prepared to accept this ending on the basis of Timmer's two arguments?

It is important to resolve this point as a group before continuing with the discussion. If alternative viewpoints surface, handle them in a way that both honors the text and the larger focus of this parable.

■ Focus 3: *The Dishonest Manager*

The second problem involves what appears to be the commendation Jesus gives to the dishonest manager. How can such a scoundrel be a model for kingdom living?

Helmut Thielicke's argument points to a helpful understanding of Jesus' intent: though God is compared to a judge or Jesus to a thief in the night, these are partial examples of their character, not complete descriptions. For example, it is one aspect of the judge's response to the widow that Jesus chooses to draw a parallel with God—namely, God's inclination to hear and act on the cries of his people.

Q. What does Jesus commend about the steward's behavior?

Q. To whom did Jesus tell this parable? How do you know?

As you discuss audience together, consider chapter 16:1 and 14.

Q. Jesus' warning in Luke 12:35-40 relates to this parable. To whom is Jesus extending this warning? What are the parallels and connections between the story of the wedding banquet and the parable of the shrewd manager?

Q. What message do these stories have for twentieth-century, North American Christians?

■ Focus 4: *Dramatization*

Through a detailed analysis that relies heavily on the cultural practices of Jesus' day, Timmer explains each part of the parable up to the point of the master's two options. In the end, the master chooses to be "outsmarted" by his crafty steward, praising his resourcefulness.

To bring these two choices and the parable itself into focus, you may wish to ask several people to act out the parable at this point in the session (make arrangements earlier in the week, to give the actors time to prepare). A dramatization of this less familiar but more complicated parable will clarify the points Timmer makes. You will need five people to play the roles (the master, the steward, two debtors, and a narrator). Encourage actors to use both the original parable and Timmer's commentary (points 1-8) to flesh out and memorize their parts; the narrator should provide commentary between lines.

After the dramatization of the parable, entertain any comments or questions that the students might have based on points 1 through 8 of Timmer's explanation of the parable.

■ Focus 5: *Parable of Crisis*

The story of the unjust steward takes place around a crisis that threatens the steward's livelihood. In coping with this crisis he demonstrates great resourcefulness. Money, which was once the object of his greed, now becomes an agent of grace. The steward "buys off" the debt of the debtors in a magnanimous gesture, drawing the debtors into pardon through an act of grace. Money no longer controls the steward: he now directs the power of money toward grace.

At first glance we are tempted to condemn the steward as a dishonest failure who resorts to buying his friends. But after a closer look, we might see something to admire in this character.

Q. What admirable qualities does Jesus' steward possess?

Q. If you were one of the master's debtors, would you have hired the unjust steward? Why or why not?

Q. What does verse 9 mean, and how does it relate to this parable?

Q. What might you have done in the unjust steward's situation?

■ Focus 6: *Dealing with Crisis*

The crisis for the steward is one dealing with his future livelihood. Jesus' assessment of the steward's resourcefulness is worth noting. Says Jesus of this man, "The sons of this world are more shrewd in dealing with their own generation than the sons of light" (Luke 16:8).

Q. In what approaching crises would Jesus' listeners be called on to act resourcefully?

Q. What crises do we, as twentieth-century Christians, face? What does the parable teach us about responding resourcefully?

This parable and the brief sayings that follow are commentaries on wealth and a condemnation on those who are enslaved to wealth. Perhaps Jesus is warning each generation about the dangers of wealth. From Luke's perspective, the wealthy will be brought low while the poor are lifted up.

■ **Focus 7:** *God's Kingdom*

This parable is about the kingdom of God. The coming of God's kingdom produces a crisis and forces a question on the listener: Are you prepared to entrust *everything* to God in return for his mercy?

The parable of the unjust steward turns the listener's attention to the last judgment (the eschaton), when nothing but the Lord's mercy will bring about a person's salvation. The steward in this parable is counting on mercy from his lord. He knows from where his salvation comes.

Q. What might it mean for us today to entrust *everything* to the Lord? Name some specific ways in which such complete trust affects a person's life-style.

■ **Focus 8:** *Closing*

Often Jesus' parables bring about a crisis that compels the listeners into action. Close by asking the group to reflect on which crises God might be using to call them into action. Encourage them to pray to God for help in determining what steps they should take to begin meeting these crises.

End the session with a group prayer or the singing of an appropriate hymn.

SESSION ELEVEN

The Pharisee and the Tax Collector

Introductory and Background Comments for the Leader

Few people will deny that Jesus was a great teacher. In fact, many are prepared to go at least as far as Nicodemus and call Jesus "a teacher come from God."

Most of us are struck immediately by the authority with which Jesus taught. He did not speak tentatively or with halting reservation. He spoke decisively and with simple clarity. People were "amazed at his teaching, because he taught them as one who had authority . . ." (Mark 1:22).

Often Jesus spoke in contrasts in order to communicate his point, to aid the listener in picturing or seeing what he was trying to teach. Jesus spoke of sand and rock as foundations upon which to build a house. The contrast was easy to grasp. Similarly, Jesus spoke of bad trees and good trees, rocky soil and good soil.

The echoes of such teachings are found in the Old Testament. Psalm 1 speaks of the righteous person as a tree that bears much good fruit while the unrighteous person is like chaff driven by the whim of the wind.

The parable of the Pharisee and the tax collector is a story which on the surface contrasts two types of people in Jewish culture, a Pharisee and a tax collector. However, there is also another contrast at work in this parable, and Timmer provides a helpful commentary in helping us to see and understand what Jesus was teaching.

Purpose of the Study

The participants will be challenged in this study to reexamine the way they perceive things and to begin seeing things as God sees them. Readers will be encouraged to pray in the light of God's Word and his standards and not to be influenced by the standards imposed by tradition or human dictates.

■ **Focus 1:** ***Hearing the Story***

Ask today's presenter to read or tell the parable of the Pharisee and the tax collector.

■ **Focus 2:** ***"Seeing" the Characters***

Timmer asserts that we need to see the Pharisee in this parable through more sympathetic eyes. Pharisees were exemplary citizens who not only recommended the importance of prayer but were faithful in their practice of fasting and tithing. They made great neighbors because they were honest and kept the law. Much of what the Pharisee in this parable prays is worthy of affirmation.

In contrast the tax collector was viewed as a scoundrel—a worthless traitor who worked for the "enemy," the Roman government. He was a cheater.

Q. Given these contrasting characters and their reputations, how would Jesus' audience have expected the story to end? Why?

In our society, as in Jesus' day, we can point to groups that we hold in high esteem as well as to groups of whom we have a low opinion. How does our overall impression of these people influence our thinking about their behavior in a given situation? For example, if a burglar alarm went off and the only two people near the burglarized shop were a wealthy business executive and a homeless vagrant, how would our overall impressions of the status of each of these individuals influence us in placing guilt?

Q. How might such assumptions prevent us from seeing the worth of individuals in a large portion of the population?

Again we should note, as in the case of the unjust steward, that Jesus neither condones the tax collector's way of life nor condemns the charitable practices of the Pharisee. Instead, Jesus shifts the emphasis toward the content of these two men's prayers.

■ **Focus 3:** *Contrasts*

What appears to others as worship of God is often really self-worship. As one commentator remarked, there are those who "get up in the morning and sing, 'How Great Thou Art' to the mirror." Our self-centeredness confuses and misplaces the true center of our worship, namely God.

We often measure our own spirituality against that of others. And to be guaranteed a high mark in this self-administered test, we tend to compare ourselves with those who appear less reputable or less spiritual. Such comparisons inevitably result in a condescending pride.

The obvious comparison in the parable is between the Pharisee and the tax collector. The Pharisee outlines this comparison in his prayer.

Q. To put the parable into today's terms, imagine that the two characters are a minister and an embezzler or a hit man for an underworld crime syndicate. Compare the two in human terms.

Q. Jesus is making another contrast or comparison in this parable. Can you identify this comparison?

The contrast in this parable is ultimately between God and sinful humanity. God becomes the standard by which any comparison must be made in the kingdom of God. What we think of ourselves and what we think of others results only from what we think of God.

The tax collector caught sight of the contrast between himself and God. In the face of God, the tax collector hid his face and confessed his sinfulness. His prayer was a plea for mercy. The tax collector measured upward.

The Pharisee, on the other hand, used the tax collector as his standard of comparison and provided God with a litany of the wonderful things he had done and the terrible things he had not done. He measured downward.

Q. The Pharisee seemed to assume that God owed him something for being such a "righteous" person. Does God in fact owe us something for keeping on the straight-and-narrow? What rewards may we expect for being obedient to God?

Q. What light might the story of Zacchaeus, another tax collector, shed on this parable?

(See Luke 19: 1-10. The point to be made is that Zacchaeus not only repents of his wrongdoing but distributes his dishonest gains.)

Q. Repentance "cost" Zacchaeus a great deal of money. Is repentance always costly? Why or why not?

■ Focus 4: *Parable as Mirror*

Parables serve as both windows *through which* we see the kingdom of God and mirrors *by which* we see something of ourselves. Traditionally with this parable we have simply sided with the tax-collector in his humility and sincerity.

However, Timmer does not allow us to get away with such an easy comparison or conclusion. Instead, he has us recognize the presence of both themes in our lives: at times the theme of self-congratulation and at other times the theme of genuine repentance, seeking earnestly for God's mercy.

Q. What does Timmer's story about the village square reveal about how God sees us?

■ Focus 5: *Closing*

Psalm 26, highlighted by Timmer, is a fitting Psalm to read together at the close of this session. Have the group read verses 1 through 7 together and then pause to reflect quietly on what has been read. Skip the next few verses and have the group read aloud three times verse 11b: "Redeem me and be merciful to me." Close with a time of silent prayer or the singing (a cappella) of the first verse of "Amazing Grace."

SESSION TWELVE

Jesus as Parable

Introductory and Background Comments for the Leader

The last chapter in Timmer's refreshing book considers Jesus himself as a teaching. To look at Jesus is to gaze upon a parable which ultimately says something about the nature of God's kingdom.

In the same way Jesus' parables function in the hearing of his audience, so too Jesus affects those who come in contact with him. There is no separating the speaker from his speech. To know the one is to know the other.

This last session will closely follow the author's discussion outline and end with an expanded time of worship.

Purpose of the Study

Participants will be invited to consider Jesus from various perspectives, each providing a parallel between Jesus and the parables he taught. Together the group will recall things learned over the course of this study in parables and will accept the challenge to act on what they know.

■ Focus 1: *Parables Are Clean Windows*

Remind the group of Timmer's point in this chapter: that Jesus is the only window through which we can properly begin to see the kingdom of God. Point out that looking through Jesus as through a window, however, can be distracting if our concern is merely with the window frame, the type of glass used, and the construction of the window itself. The following example may help focus your discussion:

> Once there was an open house that featured the latest in windows from a reputable window company. The house was located on a magnificent wooded lot with an idyllic stream running through the backyard. Many of the guests touring the house were so caught up in the workmanship and particulars of the windows that they missed what only a few saw when they looked through the windows—namely, a breathtaking view of God's creation.

Point out that likewise, we are often tempted to look at Jesus without considering what it is that he permits us to see when looking through him—namely, a breathtaking view of God's kingdom.

Q. Think back on some of our discussions on Jesus' parables. Can you describe some of the new and refreshing things about the kingdom of God that these parables helped you see?

Q. Identify some specific ways in which you and other members of your congregation can live out the truths that Jesus presents through his parables and his life.

■ **Focus 2:** *Parables Are Total Comparisons*

What Jesus offers is a package deal. We cannot break it up into parts. It's all or nothing. No one can merely accept a *part* of Jesus. To enter fully into the kingdom of God, we must accept *everything* about Jesus and what he points to. Trying to respond in part to Jesus is like trying to respond to just the nose of an approaching wild bear. We must deal with the whole bear or face the consequences!

Q. Some people believe it is possible to accept Jesus as Savior but wish to negotiate his claim as Lord. In what ways do we and many other Christians sometimes live as if the lordship of Christ is negotiable?

A total Jesus demands a total response on our part. The telling of every parable calls us more and more into responsibility and accountability within the kingdom.

Q. In what new ways might God hold us accountable because of things we learned about him through the parables during the last few weeks?

■ **Focus 3:** *Parables Are Topsy-Turvy Stories*

If you examine almost any one of Jesus' parables and hear it the way it was intended to be heard with all of its cultural moorings, it will arrest your senses. It will shock you. Why? Because Jesus wants to jar us into a realization that the kingdom is not like the world we know. Parables are meant to unsettle and change a person's existence. Parables leave the listener scratching his head, leaning inward to catch a bit more understanding. They stir the heart, making even the least adventuresome among us consider falling in step with Jesus' radical call to discipleship.

In the same way, Jesus himself is out to shock people into a consideration of the claims and call of God's kingdom. Jesus' very life kicks up the dust, kicks up our assumptions, disturbs our complacency, unsettles our naive expectations. In its place, Jesus offers himself as "the way, the truth and the life" of God's kingdom.

Timmer's assumption throughout this study has been that Jesus speaks with shocking authority and deliberate invitation. The shock comes when Jesus reveals to his listener an unexpected characteristic of God's kingdom. The invitation assumed in the revelation is this: act on this truth, this realization about the kingdom of God. To recall our study of the unjust steward, we are faced with a crisis that demands our response. Jesus' whole life and ministry bring about a crisis to which we as listeners must respond.

Q. Have you heard something in these studies that has brought you to a point of decisive action? If possible, relate your experience to the group. How might this group assist you in responding to a realization about the kingdom?

Q. If possible, decide as a group on one decisive action you can take together in response to new insights into Jesus' parables.

■ Focus 4: *Closing*

It was C.S. Lewis who beckoned his readers "further in and further up" into the kingdom of God. This is always the movement we hope for as we live out our pilgrimage of faith. Often this movement comes a short step at a time, as though we are just learning to walk. And, as in the case with learning to walk, sometimes we fall. However, there are times when we take bigger steps along our journey. These steps are often due to "catching" or "seeing" something new within the kingdom.

In this course, author John Timmer has served as a sort of guide along our faith journey. Along the way he had shown us some new and refreshing things about the kingdom of God. No moss has gathered under our feet in these days of studying together. We are not in the same place as we started out some weeks back. For that we give God our thanks.

As a concluding act of worship and as a time of bringing to a close this leg of our faith journey, let us reflect in gratitude for what God has done.

Ask the group to describe briefly those moments along the journey where they encountered something surprising or significant about God's kingdom, his truth, and his longings for people. After each person has finished speaking, have the whole group respond by saying in unison, "We thank you Lord for what you have shown to (name of person)." You may need to write this response on a blackboard or a sheet of paper.

As the leader, you will want to tell the group about something that you have learned in this course as well. Then give those participants who would like to an opportunity to offer a prayer of gratitude to God. Draw this last session to a close by singing together a hymn like, "Lord, Dismiss Us with Your Blessing" or "I Love to Tell the Story" (since this was a course about stories).

Remember to thank the group for their presence and participation in this course and encourage them once again to put their new insights into action, always with an eye toward the surprising kingdom of God.